First published 1997
This edition © Robert Frederick Ltd. 1997
Old Orchard Street, Bath BA1 1JU, England

Printed by Man Sang Envelope Manufacturing Co. Ltd., China

# *Our* Family History

## Illustrated Edition

# Tracing Your Family History

## 1. LIVING RELATIVES.

First-hand information is always the best. Your elderly relatives should be able to give you much information about their own families, their parents and grandparents, where they lived, what jobs they did and so on. Make a list of as many names as possible. They may have hoarded old documents, certificates and family photographs which will help you in your investigation.

## 2. OFFICIAL RECORDS

General Register Office: The General Register Office, located in St Cath-erine's House, Kingsway, London WC2B 6JP, holds records dating back to 1st July 1837 for England and Wales. There is no charge for searching the indexes.

You can request a copy of your own birth certificate, and from this you can work backwards, looking for both your parents' birth and marriage certificates, the marriage certificates of both sets of grandparents and so on. Once the entry has been found a full certificate can be supplied for a small fee.

Scottish Record Office: If you were born in Scotland you will need to consult the Scottish Record Office (PO Box 36, HM General Register House, Edinburgh EH1 3YY).

Local Parish Registers: For records of births, marriages and deaths before 1837 you will need to consult local parish registers which were first ordered to be kept in 1538. Not all parish registers have survived and many did not begin until the late 1600's. Most registers existing are in the hands of the clergy or locked for safe-keeping in the County or Diocesan Record Offices. Consulting these can be a lengthy process, especially in the larger cities, or if your family moved around the country a lot. However, there are some short-cuts. Phillimore and Co Ltd (Shopwyke Hall, Chichester, West Sussex PO20 6BQ) have published hundreds of parish registers thus minimizing the necessity for travelling all over the country. The Society of Genealogists (37 Harrington Gardens, London SW7 4JX) also holds many copies.

To trace your ancestors you will thus need to know which parish they were born in. You can search for this in the census returns.

## 3. CENSUS

A census has been taken every 10 years from 1801 and returns for 1841, 1851 and 1861 are housed in the Public Records Office (Land Registry Building, Portugal Street, London WC2A 1LR) and can be inspected by the general public. The census return gives information as to where each person was born, indicating which parish registers should be targeted for your searches.

## 4. OTHER DENOMINATIONS

Parish registers did not cover Dissentors, Foreigners and Jews. Sources for these groups can be found in the 12 volume National Index of Parish Registers published by Phillimore & Co. The Index includes records for the following groups: Nonconformists, Presbyterians, Independents, Baptists, Society of Friends, Moravians, Methodists, Foreign Churches, Roman Catholics and for Jewish Genealogy.

We wish you every success in your endeavour to trace your ancestors.

# The Marriage

_____

and

_____

were joined together in marriage on

_____

at

_____

_"An ideal wife is any woman
who has an ideal husband."_
Booth Tarkington

# Our Genealogy

Husband's Full Name .........................................................................................

Birth Date ...............................................................................................................

Birth Place ............................................................................................................

Father's Full Name ..........................................................................................

Mother's Full Name ........................................................................................

Brothers & Sisters ...........................................................................................

Wife's Full Name ...............................................................................................

Birth Date ...............................................................................................................

Birth Place ............................................................................................................

Father's Full Name ..........................................................................................

Mother's Full Name ........................................................................................

Brothers & Sisters ...........................................................................................

# Our Children

Name ............................................................ Date of Birth ....................

Name ............................................................ Date of Birth ....................

Husband ....................

Name ............................................................ Date of Birth ....................

Wife ....................

Name ............................................................ Date of Birth ....................

Name ............................................................ Date of Birth ....................

Name ............................................................ Date of Birth ....................

# Our Grandchildren

Spouse _____

Spouse _____

Spouse _____

Spouse _____

Spouse _____

Spouse _____

*Name* _____ *d.o.b.* _____

*Name* _____ *d.o.b.* _____

*Name* _____ *d.o.b.* _____

*Name* _____ *d.o.b.* _____

*Name* _____ *d.o.b.* _____

*Name* _____ *d.o.b.* _____

*Name* _____ *d.o.b.* _____

*Name* _____ *d.o.b.* _____

*Name* _____ *d.o.b.* _____

*Name* _____ *d.o.b.* _____

*Name* _____ *d.o.b.* _____

*Name* _____ *d.o.b.* _____

*Name* _____ *d.o.b.* _____

*Name* _____ *d.o.b.* _____

*Name* _____ *d.o.b.* _____

*Name* _____ *d.o.b.* _____

*Name* _____ *d.o.b.* _____

*Name* _____ *d.o.b.* _____

*Name* _____ *d.o.b.* _____

*Name* _____ *d.o.b.* _____

# Our Descendents

*Include further details of your children, grandchildren and great grandchildren (the meaning of names chosen, birthdays, time and place of birth, and any other special details).*

# Husband's Ancestral Chart

Great Grandfather

Husband's Paternal Grandfather

---

Date & Place of Birth

Great Grandmother

---

Husband's Father

---

Date & Place of Birth

Great Grandfather

Husband's Paternal Grandmother

---

Date & Place of Birth

Great Grandmother

# Husband's Ancestral Chart

Great Great Grandfather

Great Great Grandmother

Great Great Grandfather

Great Great Grandmother

Great Great Grandfather

Great Great Grandmother

Great Great Grandfather

Great Great Grandmother

Great Great Great Grandparents

Great Great Great Grandparents

Great Great Great Grandparents

Great Great Great Grandparents

Great Great Great Grandparents

Great Great Great Grandparents

Great Great Great Grandparents

Great Great Great Grandparents

# Husband's Ancestral Chart

Great Grandfather

Husband's Maternal Grandfather

Date & Place of Birth

Great Grandmother

Husband's Father

Date & Place of Birth

Great Grandfather

Husband's Maternal Grandmother

Date & Place of Birth

Great Grandmother

# Husband's Ancestral Chart

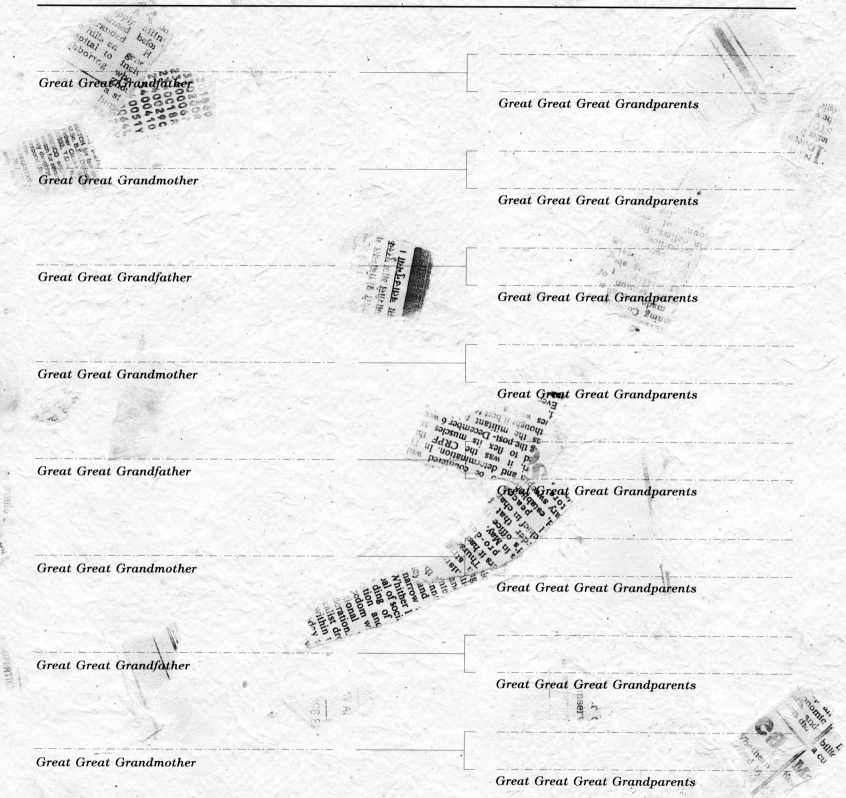

Great Great Grandfather

Great Great Grandmother

Great Great Grandfather

Great Great Grandmother

Great Great Grandfather

Great Great Grandmother

Great Great Grandfather

Great Great Grandmother

Great Great Great Grandparents

Great Great Great Grandparents

Great Great Great Grandparents

Great Great Great Grandparents

Great Great Great Grandparents

Great Great Great Grandparents

Great Great Great Grandparents

Great Great Great Grandparents

# Wife's Ancestral Chart

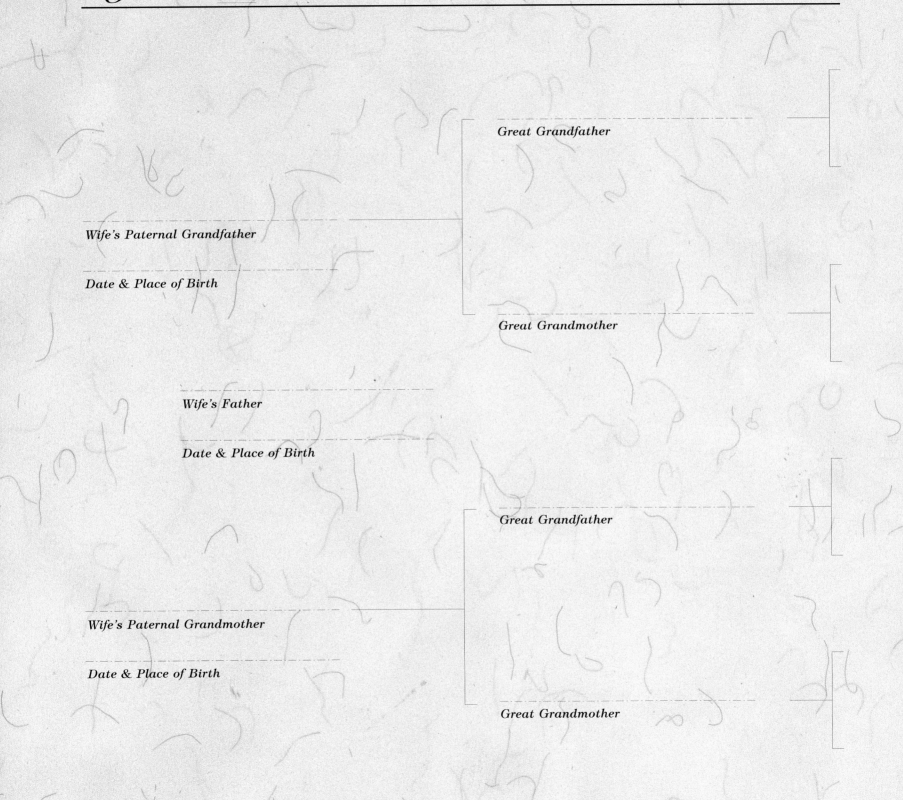

Great Grandfather

Wife's Paternal Grandfather

Date & Place of Birth

Great Grandmother

Wife's Father

Date & Place of Birth

Great Grandfather

Wife's Paternal Grandmother

Date & Place of Birth

Great Grandmother

# Wife's Ancestral Chart

Great Great Grandfather

_____ Great Great Great Grandparents

_____

Great Great Grandmother

_____ Great Great Great Grandparents

Great Great Grandfather

_____ Great Great Great Grandparents

_____

Great Great Grandmother

_____ Great Great Great Grandparents

Great Great Grandfather

_____ Great Great Great Grandparents

_____

Great Great Grandmother

_____ Great Great Great Grandparents

Great Great Grandfather

_____ Great Great Great Grandparents

_____

Great Great Grandmother

_____ Great Great Great Grandparents

# Wife's Ancestral Chart

Great Grandfather

Wife's Maternal Grandfather

Date & Place of Birth

Great Grandmother

Wife's Father

Date & Place of Birth

Great Grandfather

Wife's Maternal Grandmother

Date & Place of Birth

Great Grandmother

# Wife's Ancestral Chart

Great Great Grandfather

Great Great Great Grandparents

Great Great Grandmother

Great Great Great Grandparents

Great Great Grandfather

Great Great Great Grandparents

Great Great Grandmother

Great Great Great Grandparents

Great Great Grandfather

Great Great Great Grandparents

Great Great Grandmother

Great Great Great Grandparents

Great Great Grandfather

Great Great Great Grandparents

Great Great Grandmother

Great Great Great Grandparents

# Husband's Family

*Include details of brothers and sisters and their children.*

# Husband's Family

*Include details of aunts and uncles and cousins (father's side).*

"A people without history is like wind on the buffalo grass."

Sioux Proverb

# Husband's Family

*Include details of aunts and uncles and cousins (mother's side).*

# Husband's Family

*Include details of great aunts and uncles and second cousins.*

# Wife's Family

*Include details of brothers and sisters and their children.*

# Wife's Family

Include details of aunts and uncles and cousins (father's side).

# Wife's Family

Include details of aunts and uncles and cousins (mother's side).

"Remember me when
I am gone away,
Gone far away
into the silent land."
Christina Rossetti

# Wife's Family

*Include details of great aunts and uncles and second cousins.*

# Special Occasions

*Include weddings, christenings, important birthdays and family reunions.*

"*All who joy would win
Must share it, –
Happiness was born a Twin.*"

Byron: Don Juan

# Special Occasions

# Special Occasions

# Family Homes

"The home of everyone is to him his castle and fortress,
as well for his defence against injury and violence, as for his repose."

Edward Coke

# Education and Special Achievements

"*Education is what survives when what has been learnt has been forgotten.*"

B K Skinner

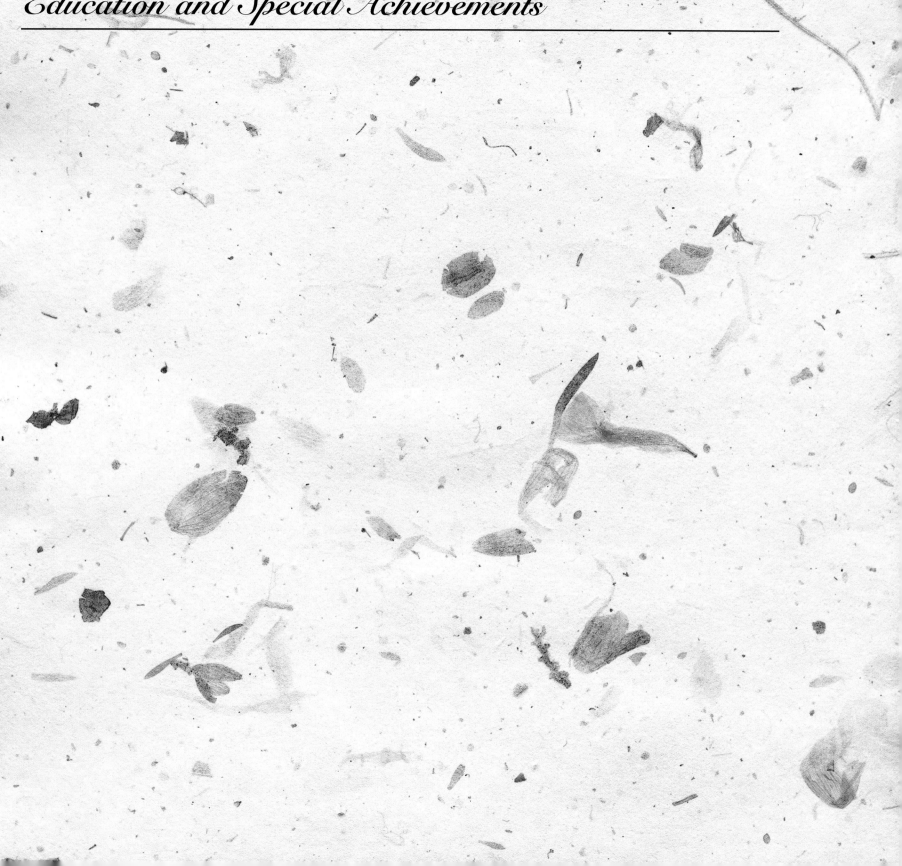

"*Whenever you see a successful business,*
*someone once made a courageous decision.*"

Peter Drucker

*"The ornament of a house is the friends who frequent it."*

Ralph Waldo Emerson

# Family Friends

# Family Pets

"*Animals are such agreeable friends – they ask no questions, they pass no criticisms.*"

George Eliot

# Family Holidays

# Family Holidays

*"What is this life if, full of care,*
*We have no time to stand and stare?"*

W H Davies

# Sporting Life

"*Sports do not build character.*
*They reveal it.*"

Heywood Broun

# Clubs and Organisations

*"I do not care to belong to a club that accepts people like me as members."*
Groucho Marx

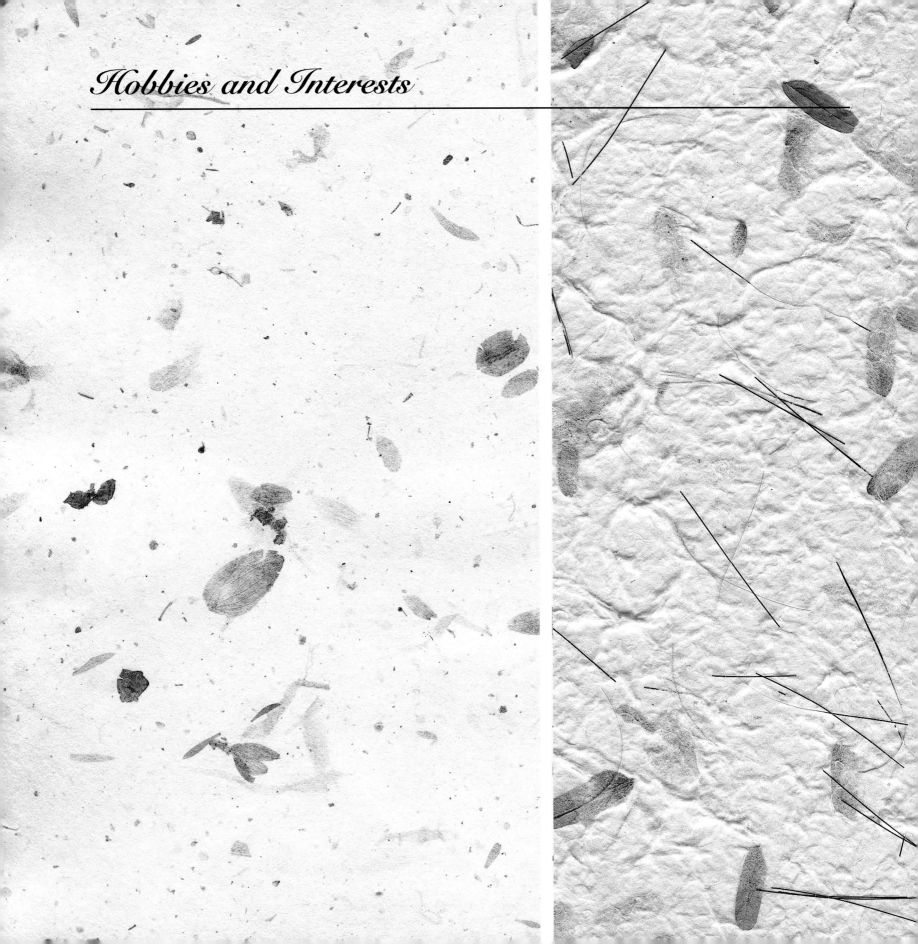

# Hobbies and Interests

"To the art of working well
a civilised race would add
the art of playing well."

Ralph Waldo Emerson

# Special Memories

Use this section for any other notes about your family, for inserting special photographs and for keeping together newspaper clippings, certificates and so forth.

"*Memory is the diary that we all carry about with us.*"
Oscar Wilde

# Special Memories

"*A man's real possession is his memory.*
*In nothing else is he rich, in nothing else is he poor.*"

Alexander Smith

# Important Family Dates

*Keep a record of your own special family calendar, including birthdays, anniversaries, traditions etc.*

| Date | Event | Date | Event |
|------|-------|------|-------|
| ............... | ............................ | ............... | ............................ |
| ............... | ............................ | ............... | ............................ |
| ............... | ............................ | ............... | ............................ |
| ............... | ............................ | ............... | ............................ |
| ............... | ............................ | ............... | ............................ |
| ............... | ............................ | ............... | ............................ |
| ............... | ............................ | ............... | ............................ |
| ............... | ............................ | ............... | ............................ |
| ............... | ............................ | ............... | ............................ |
| ............... | ............................ | ............... | ............................ |
| ............... | ............................ | ............... | ............................ |
| ............... | ............................ | ............... | ............................ |
| ............... | ............................ | ............... | ............................ |

# Important Family Dates

| Date | Event | Date | Event |
|------|-------|------|-------|
| .............................. | .............................. | .............................. | .............................. |
| .............................. | .............................. | .............................. | .............................. |
| .............................. | .............................. | .............................. | .............................. |

## Acknowledgements

pg 5 An Introduction by Emily Crawford (1869-91), Christopher Wood Gallery, London/Bridgeman Art Library, London; pg 6 Motherhood, 1898 by Louis (Emile) Adan (1839-1937), Waterhouse and Dodd, London/Bridgeman Art Library, London; pg 7 A Mother and her Small Children by Edith Hume (fl. 1862-92), Josef Mensing Gallery, Hamm-Rhynern/Bridgeman Art Library, London; pg 8 Mrs Masarai and her Daugher, 1896 by Hans Tichy (1861-1925), Private Collection/Bridgeman Art Library, London; pg 10-11 The Dancing Bear by Frederick Morgan (1856-1927), Roy Miles Gallery, 29 Bruton Street, London/Bridgeman Art Library London; pg 13 A Fairy Tale by Carlton Alfred Smith (1853-1946), Towneley Hall Art Gallery & Museum, Burnley/Bridgeman Art Library, London; pg 14 Mother and Child by Charles James Lewis (1830-92), Christopher Wood Gallery, London/Bridgeman Art Library, London; Pg 15 Mothely Love by Gustave-Leonhard de Jonghe (1828-93), Berko Fine Paintings, Knokke-Zoute /Bridgeman Art Library, London; pg 16 The Little Accident by Antal Neogrady (1861-1942), Berko Fine Paintings, Knokke-Zoute/Bridgeman Art Library, London; pg 17 Mother and Child in a Wooded Landscape, 1913 by Harold Harvey (1874-1941), Gavin Graham Gallery, London/Bridgeman Art Library, London; pg 18 Mother and Son by Fritz Zuber-Buhler (1822-1896), Christie's, London/Bridgeman Art Library; pg 20 The New Baby by Evert Pieters (1856-1932), Private Collection/Bridgeman Art Library, London; pg 21 Lullaby by Robert Gemmel Hutchinson (1855-1936)), Sotheby's Picture Library; pg 22 A Mother's Darling, 1880, by Jessie McGregor D.1919, Sotheby's Picture Library; pg 24 A Morning Nap by Carlton Alfred Smith (1853-1946), Sotheby's Picture Library; pg 25 The Newborn Child by Theodore Gerard (1829-95), Private Collection/Bridgeman Art Library, London; pg 26 The First, the only one by John Haynes-Williams (1836-1908), York City Art Gallery/Bridgeman Art Library, London; pg 27 Sweet Dreams by Thomas Brooks (1818-91), Phillips, The International Fine Art Auctioneers/Bridgeman Art Library, London; pg 29 Mother and Baby by Dutch School, (19th Century), Josef Mensing Gallery, Hamm-Rhynern/Bridgeman Art Library, London; pg 30-31 The Bleaching Ground by Friedrich Edouard Meyerheim (1808-79), Josef Mensing Gallery, Hamm-Rhynern/Bridgeman Art Library, London; pg 32 On the Beach by Eugene De Blaas (1843-1931), Sotheby's Picture Library; pg 34 Breakfast Time by Norman Hepple (1908-1994), Bonhams, London/Bridgeman Art Library, London; pg 35 Undressing the Baby by Johann Georg Meyer von Bremen (1813-86), Josef Mensing Gallery, Hamm-Rhynern/Bridgeman Art Library, London; pg 36 Maternity by Beatrice Howe (20th century), Atkinson Art Gallery, Southport, Lancs./Bridgeman Art Library, London; pg 37 Mother & Child, 1901 by English School, (20th Century), Warrington Museum & Art Gallery, Lancs./Brigeman Art Library, London; pg 39 The Mother by Thomas Musgrave Joy (1812-66), York City Art Gallery/Bridgeman Art Library, London; pg 40 Maternity by Thomas Benjamin Kennington (1856-1916), Sotheby's Picture Library; pg 42-43 Helping Mother by Giovanni Battista Torrigia (b.1858), Christies, London/Bridgeman Art Library, London; pg 44 The New Brood by Alfred Provis (fl.1843-86), Hampshire Gallery, Bournemouth/Bridgeman Art Library, London; pg 45 Mother and Child, 1880, by William Oliver (1867-1882), Sotheby's Picture Library; pg 46 Maternal Care by Evert Pieters (1856-1932), Josef Mensing Gallery, Hamm-Rhynern/Bridgeman Art Library, London; pg 47 The Happy Mother by Antoine de Bruycker (1816-84), Josef Mensing Gallery, Hamm-Rhynern/Bridgeman Art Library, London; pg 48-49 The First Tooth by Frederick Morgan (1856-1927), Sotheby's Picture Library; pg 50 Mother and Baby by George Smith (1783-1869), John Noott Galleries, Boradway, Worcs./Bridgeman Art Library, London; pg 51 Springtime, Feeding the Lambs by Frederick Morgan (1856-1927), Sotheby's Picture Library; pg 53 Out of Reach, Daughers of Eve, 1895 (w/c) by Sir Frank Dicksee (1853-1928), Chris Beetles Ltd., London/Bridgeman Art Library, London; pg 54 Collecting May Blossom by Thomas P Hall (fl.1837-67), Eaton Gallery, Princes Arcade, London/Bridgeman Art Library, London; pg 57 Baby'sBirthday by Frederick Daniel Hardy (1826-1911), Wolverhampton Art Gallery & Museum, Staffs/Bridgeman Art Library, London; pg 58 The Cradle, 1872 by Berthe Morisot (1841-95), Musee d'Orsay, Paris/Bridgeman Art Library; pg 59 'Angel and Devil' or 'Playing Diabolo, The-Devil-on-two-Sticks' 1868 by Cesare Felix dell' Acqua (1821-1925), Berko Fine Paintings, Knokke-Soute/Bridgeman Art Library, London; pg 60 My Lady is a Widow and Childless by Marcus Stone (1840-1920), Forbes Magazine Collection, New York/Bridgeman Art Library, London
Other images © Robert Frederick Ltd. 1996